THE BIBLE IN RELIGIOUS EDUCATION

Robert Davidson

The Handsel Press
1979

Published by
The Handsel Press Ltd.
33 Montgomery Street, Edinburgh

ISBN 0 905312 10 4

First published 1979
© 1979 Robert Davidson

Printed in Great Britain by
R. & R. Clark Ltd., Edinburgh

14805

JKT P
(Dan)

TION

CONTENTS

INTRODUCTION

The substance of this slim volume consists of lectures delivered at the St. Andrews Conference on Religious Education in July 1977. I would like to express my gratitude for the invitation to lecture to the Conference, for the warmth of the welcome I received during it, and for the suggestion, made by some who know more about religious education than I shall ever know, that the lectures ought to have a wider audience.

No attempt has been made to subject the lectures to any drastic revision or expansion. For better or for worse I have left them more or less in the form in which they were delivered. They represent a very tentative and hesitant step into a not untroubled sea. If they encourage others, by way of dissent, if in no other way, to take up at a deeper level a subject which I believe to be of no little importance, I shall be satisfied.

CHAPTER ONE

Mapping the Uncertainties

To enter into a minefield as dangerous as that of 'The Bible in Religious Education' is daring, if not foolhardy, for one with my lack of qualifications. My own somewhat distant recollections of religious education from the consumer's angle — and it comes from a time when religious education was to all intents and purposes equated with the reading and study of the Bible — is abysmally hazy, with two notable exceptions stemming from the secondary school level. The one was a class taken by a history teacher, a very uninspiring history teacher, and an elder of the kirk — no necessary connection. He believed in beginning 'In the beginning'; so we began at Genesis 1:1 and read verse by verse round the class. Presumably the meaning of each verse was supposed to be self-evident to any reasonably intelligent secondary school pupil. It was certainly self evidently boring. My sole, and not very originally sinful, response to that approach was the quick realisation that after I had read Genesis 1:1 it was safe to concentrate on French homework until Genesis 1:31. The other was a class taken by the head of the English department, a very stimulating teacher and an agnostic — no necessary connection. He made no attempt to conceal his agnostic position, but he treated the book of Job with the same literary respect, enthusiasm and sensitivity which he brought to the study of Hamlet. He kindled in at least one member of that class an interest in Job which has lasted and grown across the years. If my consumer recollection of the Bible in religious education is, therefore, somewhat scanty, my salesman's experience in the school classroom is nil. You must not expect me to advise you as to what to teach and when to teach biblical material suitable for Primary 7, or for fourth and fifth years in a secondary school. I have neither the professional competence, the experience, nor the ability to do an Alan T.

1

Dale or a Michael Grimmitt.[1] They bat in the John Player league; I am at most an idle, if interested, spectator.

If it were agreed that the game was flourishing perhaps the spectator's comment would be gratuitous — not that that would stop such comments being made. But there seems to be a widespread recognition today that the game is far from flourishing. Even when we have moved from a bible-centred curriculum — the effectiveness of which was seriously questioned by Harold Loukes in the mid sixties[2] — there is still basic uncertainty as to how the Bible can or should be used within the context of religious education. Noting the change to thematic teaching the Millar Report comments 'there is a danger of the Bible often being dragged in to support some slender theme. It certainly raises the whole problem of the place of the Bible in religious education and of how it ought to be used. In this context there is a need for teachers and colleges of education to experiment with their methods and it is very important that all kinds of help, critical, scientific, historical and theological should be given to the teacher.'[3] This seems to suggest that the basic need is to experiment with *methods* of presenting biblical material. I suspect that this may be self defeating unless we are first prepared to ask more fundamental questions and to try to clarify in our minds *what* it is we are committed to teach. Much time and thought have been devoted in recent years — and rightly devoted — to analysing the needs, the psychological and mental development of the consumer in the religious education field, but as J. W. D. Smith reminds us in a different context, '. . . the educational process needs two focal points not one. If we neglect the pupil and his needs knowledge may be acquired and pupils pay lip service to adult traditions, but the knowledge will remain on the surface of their minds and the traditions will be forgotten in other environments. . . . But there is the opposite danger. If we do not pay sufficient attention to adult knowledge and tradition dialogue in the classroom may become mere aimless chatter in which the blind lead the blind.'[4] Chatter about the Bible can be just as aimless as any other kind of chatter, especially if we do not pay sufficient attention to the fundamental questions such as 'What is the Bible?' 'How does it function within the believing community?'; 'How may it function in a community such as the school which cannot be identified with the believing community?'

In a recent interview Edwin Cox, who has contributed significantly to the contemporary debate on religious education,[5] was asked 'Can you give any examples of imaginative use of the Bible in schools? How is the Bible made use of?' He replied: 'This is usually badly done. Teachers still plough through Hebrew history without helping their classes to see how the Hebrews saw their history as God-guided. Bible teaching so often gets mixed up with the names of tribes. I wish I could produce an example of how the Bible is well used.'[6] If this seems unduly pessimistic let me say from personal experience that the students we encounter in the Faculties of Divinity who come directly from school — and presumably they come from the more intelligent and more religiously interested section of the school population — come with scant information about the Bible, particularly the Old Testament, and with even less appreciation of its overall religious significance.

If I may pursue the metaphor, part of the reason why the game is being played so badly is that there seems to be no agreement as to what the rules of the game are. There is abundant evidence of confusion in the two key elements in our theme; (i) religious education and (ii) the Bible.

(i) *Religious Education*

The debate on the aims and methods in religious education has taken place until recently mainly outside Scotland, notably in England and on the North American continent. *Common Ground*: A Report of a Religious Education Forum held in the Dundee College of Education, Nov. 5th–6th 1976, is therefore doubly welcome, both as a distinctively Scottish contribution to the debate and as showing that in a search for 'Common Ground' the conflicting standpoints, which have been defended elsewhere, are here in our midst.

At the one extreme we have what may be described as the *confessional approach*. One of the clearest statements of this approach comes from an association of Roman Catholic

3

teachers in Newfoundland. They define the task of the teacher of religious education as being twofold:

(a) to impart knowledge and understanding of the subject;
(b) to be 'a catechist whose prime responsibility is to share his faith and his moral principles with his students. He must not just expound the teaching of Christ to his students, but he must lead them to him.' And for this task it is imperative 'That the religious teacher hold a firm belief in an unchanging God whose voice on earth is the Church'.[7]

While this statement comes from within a church school situation, there are many who would wish to approach religious education from fundamentally the same stance within the state school system in Scotland today. Thus 'The nature and the aims of religious education can best be served by informing it with a Christian content, giving it a Christian context and basing it upon the Bible as its text and source book'.[8] The school therefore cannot adopt a neutral position; it 'has to accept its responsibility to be one of the agents of moral and spiritual renewal', a radical renewal 'which is the reaffirmation of our roots in a Biblical and Christian source and tradition'. The corollary of this is that the teacher 'has to have at least a respect and sympathy for the Christian faith'.[9] The language here is different, slightly more modest, but it is still openly confessional in approach. This approach, of course, may be consistent with raising fundamental questions about how the Bible ought to be taught. However critical Ronald Goldman may be of what has been traditionally taught in schools about the Bible, his own thoroughly child-centred approach to religious education is based on the conviction that 'Christianity should be taught because it is true: because it answers the deepest needs of human nature, and without knowledge of the love of God and a relationship with him men and women will lead impoverished lives'.[10]

At the other end of the spectrum there is to be found what we may describe as the *phenomenological approach*. It appears in many different forms. It may be defined as 'Making children intelligent about religion in whatever form they meet it'.[11] This may be pursued in terms of Ninian Smart's six dimensional approach to religion, analysing it in terms of its doctrinal, mythical, ethical, ritual, experiential and social dimensions. In such terms the task of religious education is twofold: (a) objectively and fairly to describe the traditional religions of the world, and the contemporary 'ideologies and systems which resemble and challenge the religions',[12] e.g. Marxism, and (b) more generally to focus attention upon basic religious questions about the ultimate meaning and values in life, questions to which all the traditional religions, each in different ways, provide answers. Thus the American constitution can be invoked to justify 'teaching about religions' in state schools, but not 'teaching religion'; or in James Thrower's words 'one does not teach any *one* belief, but teaches about beliefs'.[13] The extent to which such a desire for neutrality can be taken was brought home to me by a Professor in a New York College who, when teaching a course on biblical literature, by agreement with the class, never used the word God but always referred to G-D. In this setting the task of the teacher of religious education must be described quite differently. The ideal has been put thus: 'If the teacher could adopt the attitude of a shopkeeper with wares in his window for customers to examine, appreciate and even "try on" but not feel under any obligation to buy, then many of the educational problems connected with religious education would disappear'.[14] Or as *The Fourth R.* puts it 'To press for acceptance of a particular faith or belief system is the duty and privilege of the Churches and other similarly religious bodies. It is certainly not the task of a teacher in a county school. If the teacher is to press for any conversion it is conversion from a shallow and unreflecting attitude to life. If he is to press for commitment, it is commitment to the religious quest, to that search for meaning, purpose, and value which is open to all men.'[15] Such a 'conversion' or 'search' could well be described as the goal of any worthwhile process of education.

The range of possible stances between the strictly confessional and the strictly phenomenological approaches is limitless; nor is it my intention to take up one stance over against another, though my prejudices may well become only too clear. The argument here is not, of course, between a wholly biblical centred and a non-biblical approach. Even those who are most insistent upon a phenomenological

5

approach and the pluralism of contemporary society would grant that in Scotland it makes sense to give 'pride of place . . . to historic forms of the Christian religion'[16] and to examine the biblical roots from which the various forms of Christianity have sprung. The issue is not whether to use the Bible, but how much weight to give to it, and in what context to interpret it. From the confessional standpoint the Bible will almost inevitably be presented as some kind of authority for faith and conduct. In whatever language this is couched, it will be presented as a definitive revelation of the one living God, and to this extent making a unique claim to truth such as would not be granted to the Koran or the Upanishads or The Thoughts of Chairman Mao, however interesting or valuable these writings may be. From the phenomenological point of view the Bible will be treated as one among many sacred scriptures, and the attempt will be made to show children, by selected passages, the importance which such scriptures have and the reverence in which they are held in the various religious communities. This does not mean that the handling of individual biblical passages must necessarily be different in terms of these different approaches. I do not see why Nathan's parable to David (2 Sam. 12 : 1–12) or the parable of the Good Samaritan (Luke 10:25–37) should not be taught in a broadly similar way from both standpoints. What will be different is the total context in which the Bible is placed and the overall attitude to it — and context and attitude are vitally important in our approach to the Bible, as indeed they are to any sacred scriptures.

Context and attitude, with their inevitably subjective overtones, are not only important, they are unavoidable in any discussion of the Bible and religious education. In a laudable attempt to defend religious education against the charge of being merely indoctrination, appeal is sometimes made to a kind of objectivity which is not only unattainable but undesirable. Indoctrination is a highly emotive word. A helpful discussion of the various meanings of the word indoctrination in the context of education will be found in Basil Mitchell's contribution to *The Fourth R*, Appendix B, pp. 353–358. In introducing the concept of objectivity I realise I am stirring up a hornet's nest of problems, philosophical and otherwise, which I claim no competence to handle. Let me, however, venture this comment. It seems to me extremely ironic, and perhaps a sign of failure of nerve, that we should try to justify religious education on grounds of objectivity when many other disciplines are increasingly prepared to admit the necessarily subjective element in their approach. This has long been recognised in historical study. There are good and bad historians. One of the marks of the competent historian will be the extent to which he aims at a certain kind of objectivity, making himself aware of the data available to him in his chosen period and allowing such data to shape his conclusions. But no historian, however eminent, would claim total objectivity for his account of a particular period in history; and if he did he would soon find other historians who would hotly dispute the claim. A leading American political scientist puts the issue this way: 'The myth that research can be value-free or neutral dies hard. . . . To what extent are our errors, omissions and interpretations better explained by reference to our normative pre-suppositions than to ignorance, technical inadequacy, lack of insight, absence of appropriate data and the like? Today the hazards of neglecting our normative pre-suppositions are only too evident.'[17] Or this from an educationalist: 'It is often insinuated that unless the teacher can be value-free he will impair the objectivity of his research and unduly impose upon his students. But no one is value-free. No one could be. Indeed no one should be if he is to preside over the wonder and inquiry of young minds.'[18] It would be extremely odd if in the field of religious education we were to try to defend a value-free approach which has been found wanting in other disciplines.

(ii) *The Bible*

When we turn to the Bible we find, I think, the same kind of confusion as to the rules of the game and how we ought to play it. Some might want to deny this and say 'there is no problem here; the Bible is the Word of God, the supreme rule for faith and conduct', and others would add 'yes, and an inspired, infallible document'. Even if we granted this it would provide us with a general *attitude* towards the Bible, but hardly clear guidance as to how to use or to teach it. The history of sectarianism across the centuries and of the Protestant churches since the Reformation makes abundantly clear that the more people insist upon the Bible as the Word of God, the more indeed they stress its infallibility, the more likely they are to disagree about its precise meaning and the way in which it is intended to shape our conduct; and the more likely they are to insist that those who disagree from them as to its precise meaning are misinterpreting it. Further, there are many people today within the Christian community — and they extend far beyond the ranks of the Anglican theologians who produced *The Myth of God Incarnate* — who are raising fundamental questions about the authority and status of the Bible and of the way in which it ought to function in the life of the believing community.[19] To attempt to analyse the various influences which have led many people to this state of questioning would be beyond the scope of this discussion — even if I were certain what they are. I want to direct your attention to one factor only, and it is this. Increasingly we are being forced to recognise the immense *cultural gap* between the political, social and intellectual world in which we live, and that out of which the Bible comes. This cuts far deeper than we are often prepared to admit. I am not talking about surface differences, however important they may be; such as the fact that in Jesus' day it took longer to travel the seventeen miles from Jerusalem to Jericho than it takes us to fly from Prestwick to New York, and the journey was more dangerous. Even this fact, however, might make us pause and face the problem of transposing the predominantly restricted village ethos of so much of the Bible into the ethos of the 'Global Village' which is our world. Nor am I merely talking about sociological differences, such as the status of women in society, the structures of family life, or forms of government, or the character of war, however important these issues may be. There is from the religious standpoint a more fundamental problem which we must face and with which we must come to terms if we are to use the Bible intelligibly in religious education. Let me illustrate what I mean by way of an example. In spite of the exciting discoveries made by archaeology in our generation, e.g. the Dead Sea Scrolls, the Nag Hammadi documents, and more recently the discoveries

8

at Elba in North Syria, it is arguable that from the religious point of view one of the most interesting extra-biblical pieces of evidence we possess was discovered by a missionary in Transjordan in 1868, an inscription on a slab of black basalt, which we now know as the Moabite Stone.[20] It was erected to celebrate the deeds of a Moabite king called Mesha. We meet with Mesha in the Old Testament in 2 Kings 3:4–5 'Mesha, king of Moab, was a sheep breeder, and he used to supply the king of Israel regularly (i.e. by way of tribute) with the wool of a hundred thousand lambs and a hundred thousand rams. When Ahab died, the king of Moab rebelled against the king of Israel.' The date is round the middle of the 9th century B.C., and the Moabite Stone celebrates from the Moabite point of view successful rebellion against Israel. Politically the Moabites and the Israelites may be at daggers drawn, but religiously they share certain common assumptions. From the Moabite Stone we learn that:

(a) The Moabites had their own tribal or community god called Chemosh, just as the Israelites had their god Yahweh. Moreover, the relationship between Chemosh and Moab was in certain respects similar to the relationship between Yahweh and Israel.

(b) Thus Chemosh spoke to Mesha and gave him specific commands to attack certain Israelite-held border towns. 'Chemosh said to me, "Go down, fight against Hauronan"; and I went down.' In similar fashion Yahweh said to David: 'Go to Keilah; and I will give the Philistines into your hands'. So David and his men went to Keilah (1. Sam. 23:4f.).

(c) Chemosh could be angry with the Moabites, just as Yahweh could be angry with the Israelites. Military failure or disaster was attributed to such divine anger, just as military success was attributed to Chemosh or Yahweh's intervention on behalf of his people.

(d) Moab's wars were regarded as 'holy wars', and in the event of victory the captured city was 'put under the ban', offered as a sacrifice to the god Chemosh who had granted victory; just as Joshua, for example, put the city of Jericho under such a ban (Josh. 6:21).

Any adequate discussion of Moabite and Israelite religion would have to consider the differences between them and why

9

it was that Moabite religion proved sterile while Israel's faith is continuingly creative; but the similarities are striking. Even more striking, surely, is the fact that the very points which the old Testament and the Moabite documents have in common religiously, are *precisely the points which we do not share with them.* We do not normally assume that each small community has its own personal god. Political leaders today do not normally preface their policy decisions by saying 'God said to me' — and I doubt whether either the T.U.C. or the C.B.I. would be in the least impressed if the Chancellor of the Exchequer tried it. Nor do we naturally attribute the failure of national policies to the anger of a god. A. J. P. Taylor is hardly likely to talk in such terms when he discusses 'War Games' on television. We would be surprised if he did. Although the 20th century has witnessed and continues to witness atrocities in the light of which some of the more bloody Old Testament or Moabite incidents pale into insignificance, few would attempt to justify such actions as the product, the inevitable product, of a 'Holy War'; and few of us would be prepared to defend the view that the Six Day War between Israel and Egypt should be thought of in terms of such a 'Holy War'.

In the light of this, the nagging question can hardly be ignored; how much of the religious outlook in the Old Testament is simply rooted in the common assumptions of a world and a culture which have long since passed away? If this is not the natural way we think — or can think — in what sense can the Old Testament be presented as a model for our religious beliefs or our way of conduct? I have taken this illustration from the Old Testament because this is the field in which I feel most at home, but the same principle applies to much of the New Testament. Indeed there are certain respects in which the New Testament world is even more strange. For example, illness in the Old Testament is not normally attributed to demon or spirit possession, but in the New Testament, and in the world out of which the New Testament comes, certain types of illness are normally attributed to such possession. In spite of the increasing interest in the occult in modern society, we would not expect a doctor to diagnose a case of epilepsy as spirit-possession; we would not expect him to treat it on that basis, nor would we feel that our faith was offended because he didn't.

One further illustration of the problem as I see it. When we read in Gen. 12:1 'The LORD said to Abram, "Leave your own country, your kinsmen, and your father's house, and go to a country I will show you"', what do we think this means? What kind of language is being used here; what kind of experience does it enshrine? Are we to think of Abram literally hearing a voice which he somehow recognised as the voice of the LORD, a new god to him? Or, to echo the words of *The Fourth R*, already quoted, was this the point at which Abram experienced a 'conversion from a shallow and unreflecting attitude to life', his 'commitment to the religious quest and to that search for meaning and value which is open to all men'; if so, how did it happen? Or does it mean that one day Abram had a hunch that he ought to emigrate in search of a new life . . . or did his conscience tell him that he ought to pack his bags . . . or what? How do we translate the words of Gen. 12:1 in terms of our experience? Should we try to translate them at all? If we decide not to translate them, do we realise the yawning chasm that separates that kind of statement from the experience of people today, and not least the children in our school? One can sympathise with the lady who emerged from the cinema after Cecil de Mille's spectacular *The Ten Commandments* and said 'Aye, that's what religion ought to be like'; but mysterious comets chiselling commandments into the rock and tiny figures scurrying dry-shod across a sea bed with towering cliffs of menacing water on either side, are precisely what religion is not like, even for religious people today. And it is no use trying to convince pupils that it is, or that it ought to be.

From this cultural gap, let us now turn to look at a question we touched upon generally in looking at religious education. To what extent can any of us claim 'objectivity ' in our presentation of biblical material? — a question that we must face whether we approach the Bible as a 'conservative evangelical' or a 'liberal' or a 'humanist' or with any other label we are pleased to fix upon ourselves or other people. If, as has been neatly said 'objectivity means telling it as it really is, as against telling it as people think it is', [21] then I am not sure

11

what sense, if any, this kind of objectivity makes to me in my handling of the Bible. What would it mean to 'tell the Bible as it really is' in contrast to 'telling it as people think it is'? Of course, there are many people, often otherwise intelligent people, who hold views about the Bible which are patently nonsense and can be shown to be nonsensical by any reasonable study of the text in the original languages or by a study of the history of the Bible, but what do we do when two equally eminent and equally well-equipped Old Testament scholars produce 'Theologies of the Old Testament' or 'Studies of the Book of Proverbs' which in presentation, content, and conclusions are radically different from each other, or when New Testament scholars do the same with the Gospel of Mark? Which is 'telling it as it really is'? The text they handle is the same; the critical tools they use may be the same; all would claim to be aiming at seeing the text 'as it really is'. To what extent must we be prepared to admit that their different conclusions are rooted in certain personal limitations, presuppositions or prejudices, theological or otherwise, of which they themselves may not be fully aware, but which inevitably influence the way in which they handle the text? And can it ever be otherwise for any of us?

Let me point up the issue by an example from a different field. On the 6th of February 1977, the B.B.C. in its Anno Domini series screened an interview between Enoch Powell and Colin Morris. The following week The Listener carried the the following letters under the heading *That Powell Interview*:

(1) 'How fortunate we are to have an excellent interviewer such as Colin Morris, who had the difficult task of 'interviewing' Enoch Powell on 6 February (*The Anno Domini Interview*, B.B.C. 1).

Mr. Powell is sowing the seeds of hate and distrust between different cultures. His Christian thinking is warped; it seems all right to love an individual as long as he remains where he is. What about all the 'white' people who visited other countries, settled and thus formed the empire of which he is in no doubt proud? . . .

All praise to Colin Morris for a very humane, well-

12

worded interview — who gave Enoch Powell every
chance to truly say what he meant. I am afraid he did!

(2) *Disgraceful*
I have just listened to the interview between Mr. Enoch
Powell and Mr. Colin Morris. Truly disgraceful treatment
was meted out to this statesman. Whether he is right or
wrong we were not allowed to hear his beliefs and
reasons. We were treated to long and irrelevant statements by an exceedingly rude interviewer. Could we not
hear Mr. Powell again, interviewed by someone who has
the grace to let him finish his sentence and complete his
profound reasoning?'

You may be pardoned for thinking that these two letters
were talking about two different interviews or at very least
about two different Colin Morrises. Which is 'telling it as it
really is'? Perhaps neither, you may say, so let's look at a tape
of the interview and see it as it was. But even then can you do
anything other than 'tell it as you see it', which may be
different from the way I see it?

If we may return to the Bible, the problem is even more
complex, since not only do we see the text through whatever
spectacles we are wearing, but the text itself is often describing
events or incidents from a variety of different perspectives in
the light of different presuppositions there in the minds of the
different writers.

Not least is this true when we look at what must be central to
Christian belief, the witness to Jesus in the Gospels. There is
no one such witness, no one 'telling it as it really is'. There are
varied witnesses, Marcan, Matthean, Lucan and Johannine,
all telling it from their own distinctive standpoints, and on
many issues — and issues of importance — their standpoints
differ. One illustration of the significance of this will be found
on pp. 46–48. What is true of the life of Jesus is equally true of
other parts of the Bible. Attempts to state, for example, what
happened at the Exodus or to present a portrait of David run
up against similar problems; different traditions all 'telling it
as they see it'. The biblical scholar is hardly likely to claim a
certain kind of cold objectivity for his sources.

One school in Alberta, run by a particular Christian sect,

when asked to describe briefly the content and aims of religious education, replied 'The Bible and our interpretation of it'. There is a refreshing honesty about this. It serves to remind us of an issue which we cannot avoid.

If then there is today a real measure of uncertainty over the rules of the game in religious education, and equally uncertainty over the status of the Bible and how we ought to interpret it, we raise complex and difficult issues when we turn to ask, 'How can, how ought, the Bible to function in the context of religious education in schools?'.

CHAPTER TWO

The Bible — Literature or Canon?

Let me begin by recalling my own one positive experience of religious education in school, the study of the Book of Job under the guidance of an excellent English teacher who, although he had no real sympathy with the religious stance of the Bible, nevertheless saw in Job an example of great literature, timeless because it was wrestling with one of the perennial mysteries of human experience, memorable because it did so in language rich in the vividness of its imagery. The structure of the book might be puzzling; the relevance of the divine speeches in chapters 38–41 to what had gone before far from clear, but even a fifth year schoolboy could sense the dramatic impact as God turned to address Job:

Who is this whose ignorant words
   cloud my design in darkness?
Brace yourself and stand up like a man:
I will ask questions, and you shall answer.
Where were you when I laid the earth's foundations?
Tell me if you know and understand. (38:2–4)

Why should this not provide us with the key to the use of the Bible in religious education? Should we not be presenting the Bible in literary terms as 'study material for the world as a whole, and not for the church only: it is work for schools, education colleges and universities, for historians and literary scholars, as well as for clergymen and theologians'.[1] In other words, should we not have a slot within the religious education curriculum which we would label simply as 'The literature of the Bible' — studied and appreciated as literature.

A strong case can be made for supporting this approach.

1. It should be obvious that this is how the Bible, particularly in the Authorised Version, has functioned and does function in the English-speaking world. It has been a creative source of images, idioms, and everyday sayings: 'the

mark of Cain', 'the prodigal son', 'an eye for an eye', 'the labourer is worthy of his hire', 'am I my brother's keeper?'. It has been a fertile seed-bed of literary inspiration. The continuing vitality of biblical themes is amply attested in modern literature, drama and music, ranging all the way from T. S. Eliot to William Golding's 'Lord of the Flies', through 'Joseph and the Amazing Technicolor Dream Coat' to Schönberg and grand opera — not to mention Burt Lancaster's somewhat puzzled-looking Moses and a long and easily forgettable stream of Hollywood biblical epics. Is it not then culturally rather odd if pupils leave a secondary school knowing something at least about Hamlet and Macbeth, but little or nothing about Esther and Job? We might encourage them to read 'the book of the film'; they might even be stimulated to enjoy it — or at least parts of it — as literature. It would certainly do them no harm if later they became addicts of some of the more erudite crossword puzzles.

2. This approach might enable us to side-step, or at least minimise, some of the more contentious issues in religious education, and indeed in the study of the Bible in general.

We have learned to see the Bible as a collection of books, very varied in style and in literary character. Most of us would be prepared to recognise that there are books in the Bible, and sections within books, which we can only appreciate properly if we handle them not as statements of historical fact but as examples of fiction (for example Jonah, Esther) or poetry (Song of Songs, Lamentations) or poetic drama (Job) or myth in the sense of story material designed to communicate insights into human experience (the Garden of Eden) or parable. But why should we not go further and treat the Bible *as a whole* simply as literature, without raising any questions as to its factual or historical reference?[2] Would it make any difference to its impact if we approached it in this way. Take, for example, the famous and dramatic story in Genesis 22 concerning Abraham and Isaac. The story is narrated with masterly restraint. The servants left behind, father and son walk in silence towards the place of sacrifice. No attempt is made by the narrator to tell us anything about their inmost thoughts. The almost unbearable silence is broken by one brief, poignant question from Isaac 'Father . . . I see that you have the coals and the wood, but where is the lamb for sacrifice?'. After Abraham's ambiguous reply, with almost chilling matter of factness the altar is built, Isaac bound, and the knife raised . . . never to strike, as the word comes: 'Abraham, Abraham . . . don't'. Consider for a moment the impact this narrative makes upon you — its tension, its poignancy, the questions it evokes from you — does this impact depend at all upon your believing that Abraham and Isaac are historical characters or that such an event once happened in the land of Moriah? Could it not be argued that such historical questions are irrelevant to our understanding of the story and to the meaning it may have for us, just as irrelevant as the historicity of a certain Prince of Denmark is to the impact which Hamlet makes upon us? Doesn't the same hold true of the birth narratives in Luke and Matthew? Watch children identifying with the story as they act in a Nativity play or analyse your own feelings as the Christmas story is being read from the Gospels — is your response to it at all conditioned by questions of historicity, or does the story qua story have the power to evoke from you, as it certainly does from children, a sense of wonder and giving as central to human experience? What then of the resurrection narratives? When people gather to share in an Easter service — and for some of them at least this may be one of their infrequent visits to church — does what they experience depend upon a firm belief in the factual bodily resurrection of Jesus? Would it not be truer to say that, whatever their views on that issue or whether they have thought about it seriously or not, they may find the Easter stories communicating to them or symbolising for them the triumph of love over hatred, hope over despair, life over death. Notice we are not arguing for or against the historical character of these narratives, but solely that the response they evoke from us does not seem to depend upon that character. The believing Christian community has a vital interest in questions concerning the extent to which its faith is bound up with certain events which once happened at a given time in human history, but in the classroom is there not a case to be made for reading the Bible as we might read Homer? The greatness of Homer does not depend upon whether there ever was a Trojan war, which featured events similar to those

17

described in the *Iliad*. We can leave the scholars to write learned tomes on such issues, and meanwhile go on enjoying the *Iliad* and the *Odyssey*; why should we not do the same with the Bible? In James Barr's words, 'what if we were to think of the Bible as a supremely profound work of fiction?'[3]: what if we were to teach it as such in school, allowing it at each level to make its own appeal to the imagination of children?

It may be urged that particularly in Protestant circles we are far too prone to overintellectualise our approach to the Bible; too much cursed with the necessity to try to ensure that people get hold of the right end of the stick, and believe the right things about the Bible. But it is possible to subscribe to the 'correct' formula of words about the Bible, yet seldom, if ever, read it. Why should we not set the Bible free from all the religious theories which have been woven around it, forget our own particular religious stance towards it, and allow children to enjoy it as literature which will evoke its own response? Perhaps if they enjoyed it and discovered for themselves its power, they would be in a better position to understand the claims which have been made for it.

I have a great deal of sympathy with this position. We must all have known and used commentaries on the Bible which examine verse 26b of chapter 6, discuss exhaustively all possible translations and meanings of this half-verse, but tell us nothing of the overall structure or meaning of the book from which it comes; the kind of commentary which is so concerned to trace the three, or is it four, different sources or traditions which lie behind the book, that it seems to forget that, whatever the basic raw material in the book, from a given date the book has existed as literature in its present form, and in that form has been read and appreciated or misunderstood. By itself, however, this position will not do — and that for several reasons.

(a) This approach runs into the very real danger of romanticising the Bible. I do not think that it is possible to commend the Bible as a whole as great literature, even in the Authorised Version. If we are to evaluate the Bible solely in literary terms, a strong case can be made for ignoring seventy-five per cent of it — and that I consider to be a fairly conservative estimate. That there are sections of the Bible worthy to be included in any anthology of the world's great literature, we need not doubt. From the Old Testament I would be prepared to argue for selections from the book of Genesis, the account of life at the court of King David in 2 Samuel, selected Psalms, Job, Song of Songs, Isaiah 40–55; and no doubt colleagues in both Old and New Testament studies would be prepared to produce similar lists. Much of the Bible, however, would have to be allowed to sink into well-deserved oblivion. It is surely of more than passing interest that among the material I would be prepared to consign to oblivion on purely literary grounds, is much of the Old Testament which for other reasons we tend to rate highly. Most people, for example, if asked to indicate the high water mark in the teaching of the Old Testament would opt, perhaps wrongly for the prophets. Yet apart from Isaiah 40–55, the anonymous author of which is marked off from the other prophets by being self-consciously a poet of considerable stature, my preservation lists contain nothing from the prophetic books. This for a reason which Luther long ago recognised. The prophets, he once said, 'have a strange way of speaking, as if they maintained no particular order, but throw all manner of things together so that it is impossible to grasp their meaning or to accept what they say'. Although we might want to modify that statement to point out that the problem lies not merely with the prophet, but with the way in which what he said was handed down and shaped in tradition before it reached its present literary form, it remains true that as literature a prophetic book is extremely odd and more than somewhat disconnected. If anyone doubts Luther's verdict, try sitting down to read for example the book of Jeremiah as literature. There may be grounds for an English department in school including in its syllabus 'selections from the Bible', but I doubt whether there are any other purely literary grounds for subjecting children to a diet of the Bible. Other literature from the ancient Near East, for example, the Epic of Gilgamesh, would have stronger literary claims than much of what is to be found in the Bible.

(b) Even when we are handling parts of the Bible which may reasonably be commended as literature, there are often very real difficulties in appreciating it as such, because the

19

literary conventions and images at home in an ancient oriental culture may seem somewhat ridiculous to us. There is a marvellous passage in that collection of love poems which we call the Song of Songs — good Hebrew for 'Top of the Pops' — where the woman dreams one night that the man in her life has come for a midnight assignation. She hears him knocking at the door, imagines him reaching out his hand to unfasten the latch of the door. At which point according to the New English Bible:

> When my beloved slipped his hand through the latch-hole,
> my bowels stirred within me (5:4)

Can you imagine the response that would receive from the fifth year? Nor is the situation improved by the footnote which informs us that 'stirred' is literally 'rumbled'. Of course you can argue, rightly, that this is but an example of bad translation, the literal retention of a Hebrew expression which we would naturally render in a different way in English, as do both the Jerusalem Bible and the Good News Bible. Thus the Good News Bible:

> My lover put his hand to the door,
> and I was thrilled that he was near.

But not all the problems are as easily solved as that. Tastes differ, but I doubt whether the dark-haired pin-up girl in the sixth year would be particularly flattered if the current boy friend passionately declared:

> Your hair dances, like a flock of goats
> bounding down the hills of Gilead;
> Your teeth are as white as a flock of sheep
> that have just been washed. (6:5f)

Nor would he be inclined to react romantically if she lovingly whispered to him that his belly was,

> a plaque of ivory overlaid with lazuli

his legs 'pillars of marble in sockets of finest gold', and that in general he looked like 'the Lebanon mountains with their towering cedars' (5:14–15). It would perhaps be safer, and certainly more immediately meaningful to stick to 'My love is like a red, red rose'.

(c) More importantly, no approach to the Bible in purely

20

literary terms can ever be fully satisfactory because the Bible did not come into existence merely as literature, nor has this been its main function across the centuries. It is sometimes claimed that what Christians call the Old Testament is in reality the literature of Ancient Israel. As a bald statement this is not true. On the one hand, the Old Testament itself bears ample witness to the fact that the literature of Ancient Israel was much more extensive than that which is now to be found in the Old Testament. Various poems and snatches of poetry, now embedded in the Old Testament, including David's lament over the death of Saul and Jonathan (2 Sam. 1:19–27) are said to be excerpts from the 'Book of Jashar', doubtless a kind of Hebrew equivalent of 'The Oxford Book of English Verse', but now, as far as we know, irretrievably lost. The men who edited the historical traditions found in Kings repeatedly tell their readers that if they want further information about the activities of the various monarchs, most of whose careers receive very brief, pungent notice in the Old Testament, they ought to consult the 'Annals' of the kings of Israel and Judah — and the readers were expected to have access to such annals. On the other hand, *ancient* can be a very misleading term. What now survives in the Old Testament covers a very wide time span. When we come towards the end of that time span, to books like Daniel and Esther, we are in a period from which other Jewish literature does survive, for example some of the Dead Sea Scrolls. What now survives in the Old Testament, therefore, is but a fraction of what once circulated as literature in Ancient Israel, how large or how small a fraction we are just not in any position to say; nor is it the whole of what has survived.

We are left facing one fundamental question: why was it that these particular books came together to form the Old Testament? As we have seen, the answer cannot possibly be in terms of literary excellence or superiority. Who would have advocated the preservation of the Book of Leviticus on such grounds?If we say, well perhaps it was purely accidental, that answers no questions and historically is difficult to maintain. We must begin by recognising that the Bible, initially the Jewish Bible, constituted what was regarded as a *canon of sacred scripture.* Let us try to consider for a moment what this means, because very often we seem to spend our time arguing about the unimportant, the peripheral questions in this area. There has been considerable discussion in recent years about the whole idea of a canon, of a fixed and limited number of books being in some sense regarded as authoritative beyond all other books, within the context of the Jewish and Christian faiths. All that we know about the history of the growth of the canon suggests that the drawing of the final boundaries of the canon was a complex process. In spite of many later attempted explanations and rationalisations, it is not alway clear why book X was included and book Y excluded. Were there, indeed, several different canons, one, for example, acceptable to the Jews in Palestine, another acceptable to the Jews of the diaspora?[4] There have not been lacking in recent years Christian theologians who have argued that the whole idea of a fixed canon, with its apparent implication that through a particular set of books God speaks in a way in which he no longer speaks, that inspiration died out at a particular time in human history, is dubiously Christian.[5] Even if we were persuaded by this argument, the fact would still remain that *historically* the Bible has come down to us packaged as a canon of sacred scripture — and that remains in spite of the fact that various Christian churches disagree as to the precise extent of the canon. We may not like the particular shape of the canon; we may wonder whether the Jewish community was right to include Esther and to exclude Ecclesiasticus, whether the Christian church was right to include 2 Peter and exclude the Didache: but it is more important to reflect upon the basic question, which is, why did the idea of a canon arise in the first place? What factors in the life of Israel, what religious impulse, what necessity gave birth to the need for canonisation of certain documents?

It has been well said 'The Bible comes to us out of the ashes of two Temples, the first or Solomonic Temple destroyed in 586 B.C., and the second or Herodian Temple destroyed in A.D. 70'.[6] Let me hinge what I want to say around the events of 586 B.C., perhaps the most traumatic experience in Israel's history, because in it a question mark was placed against much that had been creative and convincing in Israel's religion up to that point.

Some of the Psalms are our clearest guide to much that was best in the religion of ancient Israel. Take Psalm 48. Central to it is worship, worship in the Jerusalem temple. Jerusalem to this Psalmist is not merely the proud capital of a small nation, it is the city of God, the city in which God has his earthly dwelling. This, God's presence in their midst, is the source of the people's strength; this enables them to fling defiance in the face of the power and military might of the pagan world. Note how the Psalm ends, with an invitation to walk round the temple precincts, noting her ramparts and citadels;

that you may tell the next generation
  that this is God
our God for ever and ever.   (vv:13–14)

We are here in touch with a lively faith, a faith deep-rooted in the past, tested and confirmed by experience. Other nations had perished before the military totalitarianisms of the ancient Near East; Judah and Jerusalem survived, not because of military resources, but because they were the people of God, guarded by the presence of God in their midst. This was a faith for which men were prepared to fight, and if need be to die believing that

God is our refuge and strength
  a very present help in trouble.   (Ps. 46:1)

Then it happened. A Babylonian army smashed its way into Jerusalem. The temple became a charred ruin. The whole theology of Psalms like Psalms 46 and 48 was shattered. All the outward, visible props to the community's faith were torn away. The people were left facing a traumatic identity crisis, the kind of crisis that had spelt death for some other religious traditions. In Babylonian exile, where many felt they could no longer sing the songs of Zion (cf. Ps. 137), they had to find new faith or vanish into a larger cultural and religious cosmopolitanism. They found new faith, by fastening on to certain traditions and meditating on certain books which, they discovered, had the power to give them new life in the midst of death, books which enabled them to face their identity crisis, and to discover again who they were and how they could survive. It was the community's search for a continuing viable identity which led to the birth of the first stage of the canon. It was that basic thrust which across many centuries gave us the Bible in the form in which we have it today. The Bible presupposes a believing community and continually nourishes the faith of that community.

This places, I believe, certain limitations upon what we may legitimately expect to get out of the Bible, and points clearly to what we ought to expect to find in it. The Bible, it has been well said, 'is not primarily a source book for the history of Israel, early Judaism, Christ, and the early church, but rather a mirror for the identity of the believing community which in any era turns to it to ask who it is, and what it is to do, even today'.[7] This means that if I were asked to draw up a scheme of lessons or teach a course on the life and history of the patriarchs, Abraham, Isaac and Jacob, I would have to begin by saying, 'sorry, I don't think this can be done; you are going to be asking questions in which the Old Testament is not primarily interested'. Abraham was remembered within the Hebrew community, stories were told about him and were shaped in the particular way in which they now lie before us in Genesis, because Abraham was not merely a figure of the past, he lived on in his descendants. In him, men of faith in every generation found the mirror for their own identity. They too often knew what it was to go out into the unknown and the uncertain future. They too knew what it was to be held by the grace of God in the midst of unanswered questions and unfulfilled hopes. They too discovered that to a man who was prepared to trust, often in spite of appearances, a creative relationship with God was possible. Abraham was their contemporary. So too with the Gospels. We cannot understand them if we approach them as potted biographies of Jesus. They are one and all confessions of faith by men who in different ways express a common conviction, that in Jesus of Nazareth they had been given the definitive clue to the meaning of human life and to the character of God. If we do not see the Gospels as confessions of faith reflecting the beliefs of the early church we shall ask the wrong questions, and get the wrong answers. Notice I am not saying that we must accept or agree with these confessions of faith. We are at perfect liberty to reject them or to think that they are absurd. But acceptance or rejection should take place on the other side of understanding, and no understanding of the Gospels is possible unless we recognise them for what they are.

When we are dealing with that part of the Bible which most of us call the Old Testament, there is another issue of which we ought to be constantly aware. Our 'Old Testament' was, and is, primarily a mirror for the identity of the Jewish community. Indeed that form of the Old Testament which is normally taken as authoritative in the Protestant churches was fixed not by Christians, but by Jews meeting towards the end of the first century to answer the needs of the contemporary Jewish community, one of whose problems was the rapid growth of a heretical Jewish sect called Christians. There is nothing, as far as I can see, which says that if you begin with the Old Testament you must end up with the New Testament; nothing which leads *inevitably* from the Old Testament to Jesus. There are certain aspects of the Old Testament which seems to me to lead more naturally and logically to Judaism than to Christianity, When therefore Goldman says that we must help our pupils 'to see the O.T. through N.T. spectacles',[8] I can only say that I wish to change my optician, preferably to one with a Jewish name. I do not believe that we should try to teach anything about the Old Testament unless we have first grasped that it is the witness to a faith which has value in its own right apart altogether from any possible relationship with the New Testament or with the Jewish interpretation of it in Mishnah and Talmud. This is a faith capable of providing a community with life in the midst of death, and of passing sentence of death on a community which sought to domesticate God by identifying him with its own religious and political establishment. This is a faith which breathes a spirituality and explores depths of human experience in the light of which much that is labelled Christian may be dismissed as shallow and platitudinous. Out of this faith have sprung directly two of the world's living religions, Judaism and Christianity, and indirectly a third, Islam.

To teach the Bible merely as literature, therefore, is to ignore the factors which gave it birth, moulded its form, and ensured its survival. And that is surely educationally unsound.

25

CHAPTER THREE

Knowing the Bible

So far we have been trying to map out some of the areas of
confusion and uncertainty in the subject, and seeking to
identify the status of the Bible as literature of a particular
kind, let us now come closer to grips with what we may
reasonably expect when we set the Bible in the context of
religious education, by asking 'What kind of knowledge of the
Bible is it possible and desirable to impart in schools?' Here I
want to draw upon a theory of knowledge which has a
respectable pedigree and has been influential in education[1];
the distinction between three types of knowledge.

(a) Knowledge *that*,
(b) knowledge *how*,
(c) knowledge *by acquaintance*.

Without entering into the debate as to whether this is an
adequate or satisfactory theory of knowledge, let us see how
far it would take us in our understanding of what we might
communicate about the Bible in the context of religious
education.

(a) Knowledge *that*:
Every discipline has a certain factual content or a certain
traditional body of knowledge or information that must be
known before we can talk meaningfully about the subject;
whether it be that the angles of a triangle add up to 180
degrees, or that French verbs of a certain type operate in this
way and not in that, or that the Battle of Bannockburn was
fought in 1314. Similarly there is a body of knowledge about
the Bible, about the kind of book that it is, about its content,
which can and must be taught. And no general talk about the
search for meaning in life or the religious quest or the child's
experience, can be a substitute for this. Let me illustrate. If we
ask what the Bible is all about, it may seem reasonable to reply

'it is about God'. But it is arguable that 'God' is one of the vaguest words in the English language. It may indicate a vague someone somewhere, the kind of feeling I have when viewing a sunset, or a big round — or is it an oval-shaped — blank, or apparently it can be a synonym for my ultimate concern or the depths of my being or the transcendent — an increasingly blessed word, whatever it may mean. Now it is quite clear to me that the Bible does not speak vaguely about 'God'; it speaks about a God of a particular kind, a God whose character has a sharp cutting edge, cutting enough to be offensive; a God, says the Bible, whose character and purposes were made known in certain disclosure situations, in certain things which once happened in the life of ancient Israel and in Jesus of Nazareth. You may believe that this God makes sense or is absurd, that he has a claim to make upon your life or that he is objectionable or irrelevant: what you cannot say is that you can discover this God by contemplating your own religious navel or gazing into the depths of your being. There is in the Bible a given content to the word God which can be grasped and communicated.

That is why the Bible looks again and again to certain key events which it calls upon the believing community to remember and to celebrate. That is why at harvest thanksgiving in ancient Israel people confessed their faith not by talking vaguely about the bounty of nature or providence, but by declaring:

My ancestor was a wandering Aramean, a homeless refugee, who took his family to Egypt to live. They were few in number when they went there, but they became a large and powerful nation. The Egyptians treated us harshly and forced us to work as slaves. Then we cried for help to the Lord, the God of our ancestors. He heard us and saw our hardship, suffering and misery. By his great power he rescued us from Egypt. He worked miracles and wonders, and caused terrifying things to happen. He brought us here and gave us this rich and fertile land. (Deut. 26:5–9)

This is at one and the same time a history lesson and a character sketch of God.

27

That is why Paul writes to the Corinthians:

And now I want to remind you, my brothers, of the Good News which I preached to you, which you received, and on which your faith stands firm. . . . I passed on to you what I received, which is of the greatest importance; that Christ died for our sins, as written in the Scripture; that he was buried and that he was raised to life again three days later, as written in the Scriptures; that he appeared to Peter and then to all twelve apostles. Then he appeared to more than five hundred of his followers at once, most of whom are still alive, although some have died. Then he appeared to James and afterwards to all the apostles. (1 Cor. 15:1, 3–7)

Paul's concern is with something that he receives . . . and passes on . . . something that can be communicated and taught.

It never ceases to amaze me how ignorant, otherwise highly intelligent and religiously-concerned people can be about this tradition. Harold Loukes in his interesting book *Teenage Religion* talks about the great burden of Old Testament history: 'a people who in the perils and bleakness of luxury and greed, and involved in the shifts and schemes of politics: that they were broken by the powers they sought to exploit; and struggled back from exile, aware that the God of history demanded their complete allegiance. In their corporate guilt and fear they refined their laws and regulations in the vain hope of manufacturing a system that would keep them morally and ritually pure: and they were held in it and lost their vitality. Jesus born into that freezing tradition took hold of it, illuminated it and released the spirit of liberty in which obedience to the will of God became vitalising and creative, instead of negative and oppressive. The forces of fear gathered themselves to destroy him but they failed, for the love of God broke out through his death, swept out through his risen life into the lives of men and spread through the world. . . . This is the story of the Bible that must be told before boys and girls can be asked to face for themselves the question 'What does the love of God mean now?'[2] The educational concern here is sound; but is *this* the story of the Bible that must be told? It seems to owe as much to imagination, or to Christian blinkers, as it does to what is there in the Bible. Is it really being seriously suggested that the love of God first breaks out in the Bible in the death and risen life of Jesus? What then are we to make of Deuteronomy wrestling with the mystery of Israel's existence and finding an answer in terms of the inexplicable and wholly unmerited love of God.[3] What about Jonah being dragged by the scruff of his unwilling neck into seeing that the same compassion and pity that Israel had found, could not be kept under lock and key in Israel's cupboard, but had to break out to embrace even the pagan enemies of Israel? Are we really to believe that for post-exilic Judaism religious experience was negative and oppressive, locked up in a freezing tradition? What then was the man who wrote Psalm 119 talking about when he said:

Show me how much you love me, Lord
    and save me according to your promise
. . . I will live in perfect freedom
    because I seek to obey your teachings.
. . . I find pleasure in obeying your commands
    because I love them.
    I respect and love your commands,
    I will meditate on your instructions.
                    (Ps. 119:41, 45, 47–48)

. . . love . . . freedom . . . joy. Strange words to come from a freezing, negative and oppressive tradition.

If we are going to criticise or react negatively to the Old Testament or Judaism or for that matter to the New Testament or parts of it, let us at least do so on the basis of reasonable knowledge of what is in it, and not, as so often, on the basis of what seems suspiciously like a caricature. If that kind of caricature can be found in one writing challengingly and intelligently about religious education, what about those who are on the receiving end of such education and approach it with a considerable degree of ignorance? If we are going to be faced with a society increasingly alienated from the church and from a faith which has its roots in the biblical tradition, then let us try to ensure that when the Bible is used in religious education it is used responsibly and that children at least grow up to know what it is they are rejecting or ignoring.

29

To say that is one thing; to go on from there and claim that therefore we should systematically and progressively teach everything that is in the Bible, is another. I accept to a large extent the criticism that has been voiced[4] that in our teaching of the Bible in schools we have sometimes taught too much too soon, and taught it in such a way that it has deadened curiosity and imagination, and closed doors rather than opened them. We ought to be giving a great deal of thought — and I know some is being given — to questions concerning what are the important, what indeed are the *essential*, things about and in the Bible that we ought to teach. We ought to be aware of the kind of distinction that is drawn, and legitimately drawn, in this comment on another discipline.

'. . . a man is not uneducated if he does not know who was the architect of St. Peter's in Rome: but he is uneducated if he does not know that in Europe during the fifteenth and sixteenth centuries there was a phenomenon which sprang from a revived interest in the knowledge of the Greeks and was marked by a new humanism'.[5] Or to take another example, we could say that a man is not uneducated just because he does not know the precise date of the burning of the Reichstag, but he is uneducated if he is unaware of the holocaust, the tragedy of the Jews under the Nazi régime. Let us apply this kind of distinction to the Bible.

I don't think that we should be particularly concerned if someone does not know that Jacob had twelve sons, whose names were . . . whatever they were; or hasn't got a clue about the details of the spotted, striped and speckled goats or sheep involved in the somewhat shady wage-bargaining between Jacob and Laban. It is however important that children know that Jacob is Israel, that the Old Testament is the story of Israel, of a community which in a strange way believed itself to be the people of God, a community which wrestled with what that meant, which often tragically misunderstood what that meant, and which in the midst of national tragedy and disaster painfully discovered that they existed to serve God and not God to serve them — and that much of this is there in the stories about Jacob in the book of Genesis.

I don't think that we should be particularly concerned if someone does not know the name of the priest at Bethel who clashed with Amos. It would, however, be important to know that Amos, like most of the Old Testament prophets, carried on a running battle with 'religion'; that 'religion', like 'God' is a highly ambiguous concept unless we spell out clearly what it means; that religion is not necessarily a good thing, that it may, in fact, blind people in their search for meaning, purpose and value in life.

I don't think that we should be particularly concerned if someone does not know how many missionary journeys Paul was involved in, or the names of the places in the order in which he visited or revisited them in the course of his travels. It would, however, be important to know that Paul was a missionary and why; and to know the content of the Good News he carried with him on those journeys.

In other words, the knowledge of the content of the Bible that we should expect children to acquire should be related to the fact that, as we have seen, the Bible is the mirror for the identity of a believing community. Everything we teach about it should have this in mind and should be subservient to it. This is the kind of 'knowledge *that*' we should be seeking to communicate; the indispensable core content of the Bible which should have an important part in every religious education curriculum in a society whose culture has been in a large measure shaped and influenced by the Christian faith.

(b) knowledge *how*:

If we may take the analogy of history for a moment — and it is an appropriate analogy since the study of the Bible does involve historical study — the history teacher, the good history teacher, is not merely concerned to ensure that his pupils will know that the Battle of Bannockburn took place in 1314 or that Magna Carta was signed at Runnymede on a June day in 1215; he will be trying to help his pupils to understand what it means to think historically, to see human experience in historical context and with the perspectives the historian uses. Similarly the scientist will be concerned not merely with teaching the laws of thermodynamics, but with showing his pupils how to think scientifically. So when we use the Bible in the context of religious education we ought to be concerned with teaching children how to think about religion, how to think about their experience from a biblical standpoint. I have deliberately said 'how to think about religion, how to think about their own experience'; the reason for this will, I hope, become clearer when in the next chapter we take a look at some of the ways in which the Bible has been approached in religious education.

This knowing *how* must, of course, have a firm base in knowing *that*. There is a certain charm about aimless chatter, feeding upon ignorance. Especially when we are in the realm of religion and reflection upon human experience the argument is only too likely to climax in 'Well, my opinion is as good as yours'. But you can hardly help people to think scientifically unless they know something about science; nor can you teach someone to think historically who knows nothing about history; nor can anyone begin to think biblically who knows nothing about the content of the Bible. It is equally true, however, that you may have a head crammed full with 'knowing that' type of information, and yet never enter into a 'knowing how' experience. There are people who have minds well stored with factual information about the Bible, who can quote chapter and verse upon almost any topic you care to mention — walking concordances, yet as dead as any concordance in knowing how to think biblically. You can be steeped in biblical language and know all the right phrases, but in a deeper sense be totally unbiblical. What does it really mean to speak about 'knowing how' in terms of the Bible? How will it differ from a mere 'knowing that'?

It is the difference between cramming biblical material, whether of a specifically factual or of a more general nature, into children and eliciting from them an understanding of, and an attitude to life which has its roots in, and is shaped by, the Bible. We may, for example, teach children 'In the beginning God created the heavens and the earth' (Gen. 1:1). But that, as a package of information — assuming that it is some kind of information — is different from entering into the experience of the man who wrote Psalm 8. He looked at the night sky, sensed something of the mystery and order imprinted upon it, and responded:

what is man, that you think of him;
mere man, that you care for him? (Ps. 8:4)

32

and rejoiced in the dependence and in the glory of man. To enter into that experience means to share a way of looking at the universe known to us, infinitely more vast and mysterious than it could ever have been to the Psalmist, and on that basis whispering 'Who am I? . . .' and then daring to add almost incredulously 'you care for me'. It means helping children to see that, in spite of the fact that man has now walked on that moon the Psalmist viewed from an unknown distance, and that Skylabs now orbit the earth, the Psalmist has still something lastingly true to say about the universe and man's place in it, something to which it is possible to say 'Gee I dig that' — a reasonable colloquial rendering of 'Amen'.

It is the difference between teaching that once long ago there was a man called Abraham who came from Mesopotamia to Canaan 'put his trust in the LORD, and because of this the LORD was pleased with him and accepted him' (Gen. 15:6) and helping children to see that it still makes sense to live life on these terms, that this kind of trust is justifiable, that it can provide the key to opening the door on many of the most worth-while experiences in life.

It is the difference between familiarising children with the parable of the Good Samaritan and helping them to context-ualise that parable in their own experience and life, so that the words 'Go and do as he did' become a practical challenge to them. We may call this 'biblical educatedness'. To take an illustration from the wider field of education: '. . . what would be enough for saying simply that a person knows, may not be enough for saying that a person has the inclination to apply his knowledge in the way required for educatedness. Thus a person who reacts appropriately in a situation in which he is asked "What does hot air do?", may be said to know that hot air rises. But he is not an educated person unless he has the inclination to apply this knowledge to, let us say, his domestic situation, and thus understands why cakes cook faster at the top of the oven — and it is this kind of desire to apply his knowledge which characterises the educated per-son'. Religious educatedness in biblical terms cannot be otherwise than concerned to evoke this kind of desire, for without this kind of desire there would have been no believing community and no Bible. Because in the Bible this kind of desire finds expression in what are conceived to be personal and relational terms, we are now approaching our third kind of knowledge.

(c) knowledge *by acquaintance:*

The model for this kind of knowledge is usually taken to be not historical studies or the sciences, but aesthetic appreciation or personal relationships. If we ask, for example, how I may be said to have knowledge of a Beethoven Sonata, then there are various things which may help. I can be taught something of the history of music, which will provide me with the context within which to understand the sonata form. I can learn something of the facts of Beethoven's life and his musical development. I can familiarise myself with the technicalities of musical notation and the form of the classical sonata. All this will help. But I cannot in any meaningful sense be said to 'know' a Beethoven Sonata unless I come to it by way of first-hand personal acquaintance either through playing it myself — which regrettably for most Beethoven Sonatas is well beyond my limited keyboard technique — or by listening to it being played, interpreted by a skilled pianist. What parallel is there to this personal acquaintance in terms of our knowing the Bible?

Just because the Bible is not a series of cold statements about God, but 'the mirror for the identity of a believing community', and the story of how such a community worshipped and prayed, struggled to live out its life in obedience to God and rebelled against God, knew the assurance and joy of faith and agonised over the forces which seemed to call its faith into question, there is a dimension in 'knowing the Bible' which I shall never experience unless *either* I belong to just such a community seeking to find its identity today in the light of the Bible *or* I can have first-hand knowledge of what the Bible means to such a community, how it is used and how it functions within such a community. I also suspect that, other things being equal, belonging to such a community will take me much further than the most imaginatively acquired first-hand knowledge; and a good deal of imagination has in recent years gone into the production of material introducing the various religious communities, their practices and festivals. Let me illustrate. In the hall of St. Salvator's Hall, St. Andrews, beside the porter's lodge there stands a gong. Just by looking at it and asking questions about it I can learn a great deal about it. It is suspended from a frame. It is round, made of a certain kind of metal. Its purpose is said to be to summon people to meals. So much — and no doubt more — may be coldly and factually discovered about it. There is a different kind of knowledge, however, which can only be experienced when you pass the porter's lodge as the muffled hammer gently caresses this round metal object. The sound vibrates from it to become part of your experience, triggering off the expectations which are linked to the coming meal, the food, the conversation. And yet having passed that sounding gong on several occasions I was left with the feeling that there was more to this gong than I knew, that the porter knew this gong in a way in which I could never know it unless I could take the muffled hammer in my hand and caress the metal surface. Maybe this feeling was born of jealousy or some hidden deep-seated frustrations, but when I was given the hammer and invited to sound the gong, however amateurishly, I discovered my feeling was right. There was a kind of gong ecstacy, only discoverable by those who sounded that gong; an almost indefinable experience which could come in no other way.

Here we come up against a difficulty to which I see no obvious answer. Can this dimension of 'knowing the Bible' ever be satisfactorily communicated or experienced within the context of religious education in school? Can the school, even a denominational school, ever be such a believing community? If so, how? Does it become such a community when it holds an end of term service in a local church? Is it such a community when it gathers — if it gathers — for morning assembly? What kind of knowledge by acquaintance, or even first-hand knowledge of how the Bible is used within the believing community, can be achieved within the school curriculum? Or should we simply accept, and make quite clear to our pupils, the limitations to what we can hope to achieve at this point in religious education in schools, and say to them 'that there is more which can only be known if you belong to a believing and worshipping community'?

One final comment; if what we have been saying makes any sense at all then we must be prepared to affirm that the logic of it will apply to other sacred scriptures, for example the Koran. There is much that I can quite easily learn and be taught about the Koran and its content, but there is much that I will not, and cannot, understand unless I have first-hand knowledge of a believing and worshipping Muslim community. Furthermore, even if I could bracket out my own prejudices and values — and I am not sure that I can, since very often I am hardly conscious of them — I would be surprised if my knowledge of the Koran would ever be what it is to an Imam or to my Pakistani neighbour who conveniently keeps his maxi-market open on Christmas and New Year's day.

CHAPTER FOUR

The Bible in Use

Let us take a look now at the way in which biblical material has
been used in recent years or is being used in religious
education. I am going to ask some questions about certain
approaches to biblical material which have been in vogue in
religious education. If at points the questions seem sharply
critical, let me emphasise at the outset that I am not criticising
these approaches per se, nor the educational theories from
which they spring. My concern is solely with the way in which
I see biblical material functioning in this context. I am
immensely impressed by the imaginative sensitivity and the
creative insights which lie behind and find expression in recent
material in this field, both that produced by local education
committees and by individuals.[1] I just want to share with you
some nagging doubts that I have as one whose interest lies
primarily in the Bible.

1. Let us look first at the *Life-Theme* approach as it is
exemplified in, for example, the work of R. J. Goldman. The
theory behind this approach is that we begin — and this is
educationally sound — with the child and with the child's
experience of life, and move gradually from that experience
into biblical insights in such a way that 'Life is not used to
illustrate Biblical truths, but the Bible is used to illustrate life's
experience'.[2] Let us take as a specific example the theme of
sheep and shepherds. We begin with what we shall call
situation A, i.e. life today. Through projects, reading, visual
aids, radio and television programmes we begin to build up a
picture of the shepherd's life today here in Britain in this
modern world which is the world of the child's experience.
From situation A, we now move to situation B, moving from
sheep and shepherds in our own country today ever further
afield, back — and this is our goal — to sheep and shepherds in
Palestine in biblical times. In this way, so we are told, the child
is becoming increasingly aware of the real experience which

lies behind the religious use of the word 'shepherd' in the Bible. To understand it we need to be made aware not only of similarities between the shepherds' life today and the shepherds' life then, but also of the differences which may be reflected in the way in which the image is used by biblical writers. Ultimately, of course, we are preparing the way for an understanding of Jesus as the 'Good Shepherd', but on our journey we shall certainly want to take a look at certain Old Testament passages, notably Psalm 23 'The LORD is my shepherd'. Let us call this biblical religious use of the shepherd image situation C. What is happening here is, I think, fairly clear: situation A (the child's experience of life now) leads on to situation B (the shepherd in ancient Israel and in New Testament times), which in turn leads on to situation C (the religious use in the Bible of the shepherd image).

It may be rightly argued that this is merely a thinly disguised, if indeed it is at all disguised, form of the confessional, Christian-biased approach to religious education.[3] It has been given a certain educational respectability and seeks to sidestep the charge of indoctrination by drawing upon the child's experience. There is in fact no reason why we should move from A to either B or C. A little knowledge of other religious traditions would soon demonstrate that the Bible is by no means the only sacred scripture which uses this image. A religious quest which begins on a sheep farm in the Scottish highlands could end up in several different religious traditions. What I am concerned with, however, is not so much the move from A to B, but the move from B to C. To what extent is it true that the 'real' experience which lies behind the statement 'The LORD is my shepherd' is the life of the shepherd in ancient Israel? It is hard to break with romantic illusions. We have our picture of David the simple shepherd lad on the Bethlehem hills, leading, caring for and protecting the flock. In the moment of insight born of the stillness and loneliness of the hills, he reaches out in faith to grasp the comforting truth 'Surely God must be like this, like a shepherd, leading, caring for and protecting his people'. However attractive the picture may be, let me suggest that it is a romantic illusion, even if David did write Psalm 23.

True, Psalm 23 begins with the shepherd (v. 1.), but by the

38

time we come to verse 5 the picture has changed. God is now a gracious host, inviting the Psalmist to be his honoured guest at a banquet, much to the chagrin of all his enemies — and the Psalmist is not talking about sharing a shepherd's packed lunch in a bothy or beside the sheep. Perhaps we should be content to leave these as two quite different and separate pictures, but if we wish to hold them close together then we ought to turn to Psalm 80 which begins:

Listen to us, O Shepherd of Israel;
   hear us, leader of your flock.
Seated on your throne above the winged creatures,
   reveal yourself to the tribes of Ephraim, Benjamin and
   Manasseh.

Shepherds don't sit on thrones; kings do. Long before Psalm 23 was written, one of the well-established and traditional descriptions of a king was that he was 'shepherd of the people'. This title we can document in the ancient near east from Mesopotamian sources as well as from the poems of Homer. If one idea holds together the imagery in Psalm 23, therefore, it is the thought of God as king, the shepherd of his people, and the gracious host inviting to a royal banquet. If we ask what was the real experience which led Israel to think of the LORD their God as 'king' then Psalm 80 again provides the answer. In a crisis situation it calls the people to an act of remembrance, to go back and recall the mighty things which this God had done for the community, how he had demonstrated his power by delivering them out of slavery in Egypt, by driving out the indigenous peoples of Canaan and giving Canaan as a homeland for the Hebrews. The emphasis is upon certain events in Israel's past which are believed to be disclosures of God's kingly power and concern (Ps. 80:8–9).

   Suppose you retort: I don't find this very convincing, I still think that the Psalmist has in mind, at least at the beginning of Psalm 23, simply the picture of a Palestinian shepherd, leading, caring for and protecting his sheep. Very well; but the problem still remains. What is the real experience which lies behind this picture? Why did the Psalmist believe that it was appropriate for him, or indeed obligatory upon him, to think of God in terms of leading, caring and protecting? It was not surely by contemplating shepherds and sheep, but because he belonged to a community which confessed that certain things had happened in their history, for example the Exodus, which pointed to this kind of God. In the light of this the picture of the shepherd provides a useful analogy drawn from everyday life, an analogy pointing to and symbolising *truths which Israel believed for other reasons*, which had nothing to do with sheep or shepherds at all. To put it in other terms, once we have made the move from *A* to *B*, there is no direct move which will take us from *B* to *C*. *B* and *C* can only be reasonably linked once we recognise another factor — let us call it *X* — which, totally independent of *B*, enables *B* to function as a useful analogy. The Good News Bible illustrates Psalm 23:4 'Even if I go through the deepest darkness' by a line drawing of a doctor bending over a bed-ridden patient, one hand on the patient's forehead, the other taking the patient's pulse. Perhaps we should then rephrase Psalm 23 something like this:

The LORD is my G.P.;
  he provides me with antibiotics, he relieves my pain,
  he restores me to health. . . .

Were we to do so, we are left with the same question. If we fasten on to the ideas of caring and healing associated with the G.P., that does not answer the question 'By what right, and on what basis, should we think of these ideas as being appropriate to God? At this point the Christian will want to talk about Jesus, but Jesus is precisely this *X* factor fed into the situation, not discoverable by any analysis of our own experience or that of a G.P.

2. A somewhat similar difficulty is inherent, I think, in the *Symbol and Language Theme* approach. A very stimulating, and well-presented example of this approach is to be found in Michael Grimmitt's *What Can I Do in Religious Education?*, pp. 117 ff. The aim of this approach is 'To provide children with an opportunity to recognise the special characteristics of religious language and symbolism by acquainting them with language which is evocative, metaphorical and dramatic, and educating them in its use'.[4] The analysis and understanding of religious language certainly ought to be high on the priority

40

list in religious education. If we can help children in this area, then many of the difficulties which people have about the Bible, difficulties rooted very often in a crassly literal interpretation of biblical language, would be eased.

The theme chosen is 'Rocks, Fortresses and Refuges'. The objectives of the exercise are carefully defined; to provide children with an opportunity to

1. acquire sensitivity to the *feelings* of strength, security, reliability, dignity, awe and wonder, which are evoked by the images of rocks, fortresses and refuges.
2. discern how these images may be used as a way of talking about God, as for example in Psalm 18:2.

> The LORD is my rock, and my fortress, . . .
> my God, my rock, in whom I take refuge. . . .

What a wealth of educationally interesting material now opens up. We may begin by examining different types of rocks, finding out about their qualities and uses. We take a look at famous rock formations, learning something about the geology and history of Ailsa Craig or the Bass Rock or the rock on which Edinburgh Castle is built. We listen to poems and stories about rocks; we are encouraged to try our hand at writing such stories and poems. We look at common everyday expressions which use the word rock, applying it either to objects or to people. We consider the use of rock, for example as the foundation for castles or churches or houses. We do a project on Masada, Herod's desert fortress where the Jews made their last heroic, despairing stand against the Romans. We ask why people made buildings out of rocks — for worship, for refuge, etc. We look at ways in which people have expressed their belief about God as a refuge; the illustrations being taken mainly from the Psalms. Then we ask: 'Is this a useful way of talking about God? Is it sufficient to say he is a Rock, a Fortress and a Refuge?'

This brief summary does scant justice to the range of exciting material gathered together in this theme. It is just at the last step that I have difficulty. Suppose in response to the question 'Is this a useful way of talking about God?' someone asks '*Why* should this be considered a useful way of talking about God?': where do we go? It is not obvious to me that

41

ideas like 'security' and 'reliability', which may have been culled from our consideration of rocks, are ideas which we are under any compulsion to associate with the word god. The history of religion bears witness to many gods and goddesses who have been highly unpredictable and unable to offer their devotees much in the way of security. If the Old Testament uses this kind of language about God we must ask why it does so, why it regarded rock, fortress and refuge as suitable descriptions of God. A careful reading of the Psalms cited by way of illustration would reveal that in every case the Psalmist recalls or appeals to certain experiences or events from Israel's past which have nothing to do with rocks, fortresses or refuges, or the feelings which these evoke. But it is these experiences and events which alone make the use of such language meaningful, by way of illustration, when applied to the God of Israel. And at this point we can hardly be anything other than confessional. Certainly let us explore the special characteristics of religious language, but if we are going to draw our material from the Bible, let us ask why language of a particular kind was considered meaningful to the biblical writers and what in fact it means in biblical tradition. The concept of God as 'fortress' is by no means confined to the Bible. It appears in Canaanite religious texts celebrating the worship of Baal. This does not, however, mean that when a Canaanite used it of Baal and a Hebrew used it of Yahweh they necessarily meant the same thing.

We have been concentrating, in terms of the *Life Theme* and *Symbol and Language Theme* approaches, on the sometimes unrecognised problems involved in moving from *B* to *C*. Before we turn to other approaches, perhaps it is also worth drawing attention to the fact that it is not always as easy or as useful as it is imagined to move from *A* to *B*, from our experience of life now to the biblical then. A theme which appears with inevitable frequency in religious education curricula is the theme of homes and families. We begin with the child's experience — and this can be highly problematic, given the increasing number of broken and one parent families — and then we set out on a journey to that home in Nazareth in the light of which we may hope to gain a deeper understanding into the family language, such as 'father', used in the New Testament. But how do we make the move here from A to *B*; and is it worth making? There are two problems that we must recognise and try honestly to face:

(a) How much can we really know about that family home in Nazareth and the childhood of Jesus? The answer, even when you have gleaned all that there is to glean in the Gospels, is very, very little. The absence of hard information seems too often to be turned into a virtue, as pious imagination proceeds to reconstruct an idyllic scene. We are largely in this context, journeying into the unknown, and we ought to have the honesty to say so.

(b) Suppose for a moment it were possible to reconstruct in fair detail that family life in Nazareth, how would we move from our family situation today to that family life; and what would be the point of it? It is arguable that we would be dealing with basically dissimilar situations. Not only would we be moving from a western to an eastern setting, but we would be crossing an immense cultural chasm. Mother out working; teenage daughter dashing out to keep a date, leaving a chaotic room in her wake; record-player blaring forth its decibels; the family seldom meeting as a family except to watch the current favourite T.V. show; neighbours largely unknown; holidays in Majorca; religion very much an optional extra — what would all this have in common with a family in first-century Palestine? If we think that it is possible to move from the child's experience of homes and family to a deeper under-, standing of biblical language, would it not be better to encourage them to play out father, mother and children's roles in a Wendy house than to try to introduce them to an alien situation? Certainly to talk in vaguely pious terms about Jesus' boyhood in Nazareth is likely to be both culturally and religiously irrelevant.

3. We turn now to the *Problem* approach, as it is exemplified in Harold Loukes' book *Teenage Religion*. This approach begins with a social or moral problem which has a direct bearing upon the teenager's life. Let us take the problem of work. We approach it through a four-stage exercise:

(i) The problem is raised. This can be done in many ways. Suppose we begin by collecting advertisements for labour-saving devices; washing machines, dish washers, garden sprinklers, electric hedge cutters. One advert may depict mother and father sitting with their feet up while the machines do the work. This focuses the central dilemma — is work in fact something to be dodged?

(ii) The problem is analysed. Again this can be done in a variety of different ways. Let us ask, what gives work its importance? Is it the money factor? Is it service to the rest of the community? Is it the need to be creative? What are the problems raised by working conditions in an increasingly automated and technological society? How should society respond to the prospect of a substantial, permanent pool of unemployment?

(iii) In the light of a realistic analysis of the problem an attempt is made to give a Christian judgement.

(iv) We then try to face how this judgement should be applied in our society.

It is at the point where we are considering a Christian judgement that an appeal is usually made to the Bible. In the case cited this means, as far as the Old Testament is concerned, referring to three passages from the book of Proverbs, passages which warn against shirking or laziness:

Proverbs 6:6–9. The famous passage which begins 'Go to the ant, thou sluggard, consider her ways, and be wise' or as the Good News Bible translates more prosaically, but perhaps more meaningfully, 'Lazy people should learn a lesson from the way ants live'.

Proverbs 15:19. 'If you are lazy, you will meet difficulty everywhere, but if you are honest, you will have no trouble' — and I suppose by a slight exercise of exegetical ingenuity 'honest' could be taken to mean 'doing an honest day's work'.

Proverbs 26:14–16. 'The lazy man turns over in bed. He gets no farther than a door swinging on its hinges. Some people are too lazy to put food into their own mouths. A lazy man will think he is more intelligent that seven men who can give good reasons for their opinions.'

I am puzzled, not by laziness; with that I am only too familiar. I think I know why these passages have been chosen. They are all listed together in traditional concordances under the word 'sluggard'. At another level, however, I cannot understand why they have been cited. If this is the sole contribution which the Old Testament has to make to a Christian, or indeed a secular, consideration of the problem of work, is it worth making? All these statements are but examples of common sense, proverbial sayings close parallels to which could be found in many cultures. Similar injunctions grace 'The Thoughts of Chairman Mao' or occur in the aphorisms of Dennis Healey, not to mention Conservative Party manifestos. Do such sayings become any more significant, do they help us to a Christian judgement just because they occur in the Bible? There is further a very real danger that in this kind of approach the Bible may come to be regarded as some form of problem-solver, giving us at least the outline of correct answers if only we pick the right verses. But this is to ignore a whole host of problems raised by the nature of the Bible in its historical and cultural conditioning. How are we to jump from the man of the Bible with his problems and his situation in a culture and society vastly different from ours, to the man of today. How do we use the Bible to provide us with practical guidance on the issue of war, when in the Bible war means intertribal skirmishes or battles in which the most fearsome weapons were the chariot or the well-drilled Roman legion, while for us it is the Polaris submarine and the so-called nuclear deterrent? Or if we are asked to bring a Christian judgement to bear on the problems in the Middle East today are we entitled to assume that the modern state of Israel is in some sense the continuance of the Israel of the Old Testament and thus talk of the Six Days War in terms of the Old Testament concept of the Holy War?[5] Unless we are prepared to face up to issues such as these, then to use the Bible as a problem-solver may be a dangerous exercise in self-deception.

4. Let us now look at what we may call the *Situation Theme* approach. Here were are concerned to take a situation in which people are inevitably caught up in moral choices or decisions. We seek to analyse the attitudes of the people involved in such a situation, and try to discover how their attitudes are related to, or controlled by, the beliefs or prejudices they hold. Thus we shall help children to gain

insights into their own decision-making, and the beliefs and prejudices which influence the decisions they take. Such a 'situation' need not, of course, be taken from the Bible; indeed it could be argued that many of the issues which are present in biblical material can be most sharply focused through material which is 'non-biblical' in the sense that it is drawn from contemporary society. The Bible, however, does provide excellent examples of 'situation themes'. One which would be of obvious interest and relevance would be the events of Holy Week. We can decide to follow Jesus through the events of that week, look at what he did, the choices he had to make, and the reasons which lay behind these choices. We can do likewise with the disciples, with the Jerusalem 'man in the street', with Pilate, with Caiaphas. Let us examine the first day of Passion week; Jesus rides into Jerusalem on a donkey. What lay behind this action of Jesus? Was it something deliberately planned in advance by Jesus and, if so, with what intent? Did his disciples, did the crowds of pilgrims, understand what he was doing, and what was their response?

This is one of the incidents in the life of Jesus which is recorded in all four gospels, in Matthew 21:1–11, in Mark 11:1–11, in Luke 19:29–44, and in John 12:12–19. Without entering into the detailed differences between the four accounts — and there are many — let me draw your attention to two things:

(a) Matthew, Mark and Luke give the strong impression that this ride into Jerusalem was deliberately and carefully planned in advance. Two disciples are sent on ahead into a village to procure a donkey; they are provided with an agreed password. As Jesus, mounted on the donkey and accompanied by his disciples, approaches the city, crowds gather to greet him with words which echo one of the great pilgrim Psalms in the Old Testament, Psalm 118:25, 26, but which, in the case of Mark and Luke, have been made more explicit to emphasise a claim to kingship. John 12, however, gives a very different impression. Nothing is said of any pre-arranged plan. Crowds of pilgrims hear that Jesus is approaching the city. They come out to greet him, news having got around of the sign he had performed in raising Lazarus from the dead. Jesus, apparently quite by chance, finds a donkey, mounts it and then rides into the city.

(b) The only Old Testament passage to which Mark and Luke refer in this incident is Psalm 118. Matthew, however, deliberately goes out of his way to link the incident with Zechariah, 9:9.

> Tell the daughter of Zion,
>> Here is your king, who comes to you in gentleness,
>>> riding on an ass,
>>>> riding on the foal of a beast of burden.

So eager is Matthew to underline the parallel that he, and he alone, introduces into the narrative two animals, a donkey and its foal. The Zechariah passage in fact speaks only of one animal, using a technique which is characteristic of much Hebrew poetry, parallelism, the form and content of one line being echoed and repeated in slightly different language in the next line. The careful planning and the two animals, however, certainly suggest that Matthew believed that Jesus had this passage in Zechariah in mind, and that the disciples at least would understand his intention in this acted parable. John 12 likewise has a reference to an abbreviated form of the Zechariah passage, but only one animal. John, however, deliberately goes out of his way to underline that 'At the time his disciples did not understand this, but after Jesus had been glorified they remembered that this had been written about him, and that this had happened to him'. So according to John the disciples did not appreciate the meaning of the incident until after the crucifixion and the resurrection.

We are so accustomed to read such familiar incidents as unified stories that we seldom stop to realise that there are several different versions of the incident, differing significantly from one another. We can understand why they differ once we recognise the different standpoints, interests and religious outlooks of the different gospels. It should be obvious, however, that, by the very nature of our sources, it may not be as easy as we think to answer questions such as 'What was Jesus' attitude or intention or that of the disciples?' If we use the entry into Jerusalem as a 'situation theme' then the answers we give to questions about choices, decisions and beliefs depend to a large extent upon whether we follow Matthew's version of the story or John's. But you may say, 'Isn't this simply to drag biblical criticism quite unnecessarily into the religious education curriculum?' I think not. In outlining a 'situation theme' based upon the events of Holy Week for children aged 11–13, Michael Grimmitt lists as one of its objectives — to provide children with an opportunity 'to engage in elementary Biblical research and "Biblical criticism" and to draw conclusions in accordance with their findings'.[6] May I underline that, and plead that whatever else we shrink from in our handling of the Bible in religious education in school, we do not shrink from this? And eleven plus is certainly not too early to introduce it. What is at stake here is certainly not niggling detail but two very important issues. Firstly, it is often claimed that such criticism is responsible for destroying faith, creating sceptics who will see the Bible as just another fallible book with no authority over their lives. I would not wish to deny that this may have been the experience of some, but I would want to underline — and on the basis of personal experience — the response made almost eighty years ago by one of Scotland's greatest critical scholars and evangelical preachers, George Adam Smith, '. . . anyone who has had practical dealings with the doubt and religious bewilderment of his day can testify that those who have been led into unbelief by modern criticism are not for one moment to be compared in number with those who have fallen from faith over the edge of the opposite extreme',[7] i.e. an insistence upon the literal infallibility of the Bible. By introducing children to biblical criticism, by showing them how in the Bible, as elsewhere, evidence must be weighed, inconsistencies and contradictions explained, sources analysed, we are making it possible for them to grow into a reasonable, intelligent understanding of the Bible which can be the basis of a responsible, maturing faith. Any other approach is a betrayal of their intelligence. Any other approach is an invitation to do an intellectual double-think, with the Bible wrapped up in a pious, obscurantist cocoon which must not be disturbed by the intelligent questions we seek to encourage in other disciplines.

Secondly, what is at stake is our understanding of the way in which we think the Bible talks about God and his activity in the world. Let me illustrate what I mean by referring again to the film which I would rate high on my list of the Top Ten most irreligious films I have ever seen — the Cecil B. de Mille Hollywood spectacular 'The Ten Commandments'. If you have seen the film you will remember that when it comes to the Hebrew flight from Egypt and the crossing of the Red Sea, you are shown a vast expanse of turbulent water, lashed by some mid-Pacific hurricane. The waters divide to reveal dry land, across which the Hebrews scurry like tiny midgets while the waters tower perpendicularly in gigantic walls on either side. Any doubts you may have entertained about the wholly miraculous character of this event are drowned in the cataclysm of avenging waters which overwhelm Pharaoh's army. So we journey to Mt. Sinai and to the giving of the commandments. Out of a dark and lowering sky there flashes some kind of comet — a Hebrew comet since it writes from right to left. Into the rock it drills commandment number one. Comet two pierces the darkness to write commandment two . . . and so on. If we ask whether these events were acts of God, then there can only be one answer; of course they were — either that or they are pure fairy-tale make belief. If this is the alternative with which the Bible confronts us, then between the way in which God acts in the Bible and our experience there is an unbridgeable gulf. Maybe many children sense this gulf earlier than we think, and from then on the Bible is for them largely irrelevant, dismissed in fairy-tale make belief. But is this Hollywood version really faithful to what the Old Testament has to say about, for example, the crossing of the sea? Remember that Hebrew has no word corresponding to our words 'loch' or 'lake'. Any stretch of water can be called sea. The Sea of Galilee is no more a 'sea' than Loch Lomond. The 'Red Sea' of the narrative in Exodus can be more accurately translated the 'Loch of Reeds'. Although we do not know its precise location — the topography of the area having been changed by, among other things, the Suez Canal — it could refer to any reasonably sized and perhaps comparatively shallow stretch of water. But more importantly — and this is where biblical criticism becomes crucial — the story of the crossing of the sea or loch as it now

49

lies before us in the book of Exodus is a story woven together from several different traditions, which come from different periods in Israel's history and reflect different religious interests. It is only by totally ignoring this that you end up with the Hollywood technicolour extravaganza. The earliest tradition — if our present understanding of the narrative is anywhere near being right — simply says: 'The LORD drove the water back with a strong east wind. It blew all night and turned the sea into dry land . . . and the Israelites went through the sea on dry ground' (Exod. 14:21, 22). Perhaps even earlier than this narrative there is preserved in the book of Exodus a brief snatch of song in which the women celebrated what had happened.

Sing to the LORD, because he has won a glorious victory;
he has thrown the horses and their riders into the sea!
(Exod. 15:21)

Notice two things: firstly, our earliest sources are quite clear in insisting that what happened was God in action, winning a victory for his people; and secondly, they describe what happened in fairly mundane terms, the action of a strong east wind. There is nothing here to justify the spectacularism of the film. It is not in the least surprising that as the story was told and retold within the believing Hebrew community as an example, perhaps *the* example of God's goodness towards them, the religious symbolism is heightened particularly when the event is being celebrated and relived in worship. Thus Psalm 77 ends:

When the waters saw you, O God, they were afraid,
and the depths of the sea trembled,
The clouds poured down rain;
thunder crashed from the sky,
and lightning flashed in all directions.
The crash of your thunder rolled out,
and flashes of lightning lit up the world;
the earth trembled and shook.
You walked through the waves;
you crossed the deep sea,
but your footprints could not be seen.

50

> You led your people like a shepherd,
>> with Moses and Aaron in charge. (Psalm 77:16–19)

This is poetic, dramatic religious imagery, the language of liturgy, and must be recognised as such.

It is worth helping children to see that when the Bible talks about God in action it is not *necessarily* talking about events or experiences which are spectacular. It would not be difficult to show that most of the events in the Old Testament which are referred to in terms of God's saving or judging purposes, are events which most people in ancient Israel in every age either misunderstood or ignored. And it is worth remembering, as the gospels make clear, that most of the people who met Jesus during his lifetime either misunderstood his intentions or saw in him nothing worthy of note.

CHAPTER FIVE

A Suggested Theme

Perhaps by this time those of you who have a personal involvement in religious education are becoming at least mildly infuriated at an academic spectator indulging in gratuitous comment on what is happening in the field of religious education — although I warned at the outset that this was all I was competent to do. Suppose in desperation or in anger someone were to say to me: 'Well, if you were to be confronted with the challenge to produce a series of lessons or to suggest a theme, suitable for religious education in school and at the same time genuinely rooted in the Bible, what would you do?' Let me stick my neck out and make one suggestion concerning something which I would be very concerned to teach, certainly at the upper levels of the secondary school.

If, as we are assured, to err is human, so is to rebel; and the two, erring and rebelling, are not to be confused. At the secondary school we should expect to find, indeed we should encourage, a radical questioning of religious presuppositions, a need to take a long, cool look at what may have been uncritically accepted from home, church or Sunday school. So we may find the Bible being airily dismissed as old hat or as disproved by science; the church is an irrelevancy, and the people who believe in such things are squares. In the midst of it all, the more thoughtful are struggling to come to terms with what they can hold on to in a world of apparent meaninglessness and cruel confusion whose frontiers are none too clear. We are in the age of theological juvenile delinquency — or are we? In this situation the Bible tends to be seen as part of the tradition against which there is the need to rebel; a book of certainties, a book of revelation, comforting no doubt if you can swallow it — but suppose you can't? Gilbert Murray in commenting on Euripides says, 'Every man who possesses real vitality can be seen as the resultant of two forces. He is firstly the child of a particular tradition. He is secondly, in one degree or another, a rebel against that tradition. And the best traditions make the best rebels.'[1] Would it not be useful to help teenagers — and others — to see that the Bible itself is a book pulsating with rebels, and that the biblical tradition produced some of the best rebels of all time? If we are ever to come to terms with the Bible we must realise that 'The working out of the biblical model for the understanding of God was not an intellectual process so much as a personal conflict, in which men struggled with their God and with each other about their God![2] Let me give one or two illustrations of what this means.

1. If we think of the Psalms, whatever their individual origin, as becoming the 'hymn book of ancient Israel', then we ought to be aware of one interesting and vital distinction between the Psalms and any comparable hymn book used in church. No modern hymn book so seriously questions, probes and challenges some of the assumptions of faith; no modern hymn book so honestly draws attention to the difficulties in believing. Nearly one third of the Psalms fall into the category of 'laments', either the lament of the community faced with national crisis, or the lament of the individual facing his personal crisis. It is characteristic of such laments that they contain within themselves a continuing dialogue between doubt and assurance, between faith and scepticism, between the clear witness of tradition and the baffling ambiguities of the present. Take Psalm 73. It begins with the Psalmist giving voice to what every believer knew to be true:

God is indeed good to Israel,
    to those who have pure hearts (v. 1.)

Yes, but look, says the Psalmist, I've got a problem to which I can see no answer, a problem which threatens the very foundations of my faith. You don't need to look far to see that the world is a topsy-turvy, unjust place. It's the crooks and hoodlums who prosper:

. . . things go well for the wicked. (v. 3)

It is all right being brought up to believe that the wicked don't get on in the world, but there is a lot of evidence pointing to the fact that they do. They rake in the shekels, arrogantly flaunt their wealth, scoff at the suckers who play it by the book, and snap their fingers in the face of God.

> They say, 'God will not know,
>   the Most High will not find out'.
> That is what the wicked are like.
>   They have plenty and are always getting more.
>   (vv. 11–12)

What then are we to conclude; that the good life is pointless? Why then do other people go on believing? There are no easy answers.

> I tried to think the problem through,
>   but it was too difficult for me
>   until . . . (v. 16)

until . . . and then the Psalmist describes something which happened to him in the temple, an experience in worship which happened to him in the temple, an experience in worship which convinced him of two things:

(a) the success and the prosperity of the wicked were in fact built on very shaky, transient foundations.

(b) even if the wicked do prosper, it does not matter. The Psalmist has something that they can never have, a relationship with God which is an end in itself. That relationship is the supreme value in life even if it does not pay calculable dividends in material terms.

> . . . you hold me by the hand.
> What else have I in heaven but you?
> Since I have you, what else could I want on earth?
>   (vv. 23, 25)

Notice that by the end the Psalmist has won through to a deeper appreciation of what faith means. I want to suggest, however, that he would never have reached that point, never have seen what he did see so clearly, unless he had been forced to question, to agonise, to feel the foundations crumbling under his feet. In this, and in many other Psalms we can sense doubt playing a creative role in leading people to a more mature faith, more able to withstand the pressures that life puts upon it. It helps to know that doubt is often not the enemy of faith but a growing point in faith.

The following Psalm, Psalm 74, is a community lament. It begins with that urgent, pain-filled, often rebellious monosyllable which echoes across the Psalms, as it has echoed in people's experience in all ages — *why?*

Why have you abandoned us like this, O God?
Will you be angry with your own people for ever? (v. 1)
. . .
Why have you refused to help us?
Why do you keep your hands behind you? (v. 11)

It ends with the Psalmist pleading with God to do something to redress the tragic situation in which the community finds itself. There is, the Psalmist feels, so much in the present which just does not seem to make sense in the light of what the community has been taught to believe. He knows all about the credibility gap.

Or take Psalm 44:

With our own ears we have heard it, O God —
    our ancestors have told us about it,
about the great things you did in their time,
    in the days of long ago (v. 1)

Yes, we have all heard of the good old days of faith, haven't we; but *now*

. . . you left us helpless among wild animals;
you abandoned us in deepest darkness. (v. 19)

It is just not possible to reconcile with the harsh reality of life as we know it all that we have been brought up to believe, all that people have claimed to be true. And in this numbing soul-destroying situation all that people can do is to cry out:

Wake up, LORD! Why are you asleep?
    Rouse yourself. . . .
Why are you hiding from us? (vv. 23, 24)

Put into contemporary jargon this is close to saying 'God is dead'. Somewhere in all this we can hear echoes of what young people are saying today, can't we?

- it's a puzzling world; as far as I can see it does not make sense, there is too much injustice, too much innocent suffering.
- what is the point in believing?
- religion may be a good thing for the over forties, but it does not ring any bells for us.
- even if there is a god, there is not much sign that he does anything.

The curious thing is that although there are many Psalms of lament in the Old Testament Psalter, they are conspicuous by their absence in the Psalms selected for inclusion in Church Hymnary 3; nor are there hymns of this type in most of the hymn books which we use in worship today. To what is this pointing? Are we saying, by default if by nothing else, that worship is the place from which we ought to exclude our doubts and our questioning? This is where we huddle together to comfort ourselves with our certainties; and let no rough, unsettling intruders enter. It might be worth wondering whether this may not be *one* of the reasons why worship tends to be dismissed as boring by many young people today. It is just not where they are. But the Psalms are there, with that refreshingly healthy honesty which is sometimes lacking in our liturgical material.

2. Let us take a look for a moment at the great prophets of Israel. It is very easy to get the wrong impression, the impression which is well summed up in this description of prophetic thinking as being grounded in 'mystical revelation and the religious attitude produced by dependence on it. . . . They (i.e. the prophets) were perfectly sure: and on their perfect sureness they built up their system.'[3] Read one of the prophetic books, for example Amos, and this is the impression that you tend to get: 'Thus says the LORD' is the prophet's signature tune, and this seems to leave little room for argument and even less for doubt. But this is a misleading impression based in part upon the way in which the teaching of the prophets has been handed down to us. A prophet like Amos or Isaiah was primarily important in the eyes of those who preserved his memory and cherished the tradition of his ministry because of the 'word' communicated by him to the community on the authority of God. Such people did not

share our modern interest in prophetic psychology. Indeed if you ask what we really know about the inner life of most of the Old Testament prophets, the answer can only be 'very little'. The notable exception to this is Jeremiah. Embedded in the book of Jeremiah there is a series of passages which have been described as his 'Confession' or his 'Personal Diary'. These passages are closely modelled on the Psalms of lament, but bear the mark of an intense individuality. For a moment the veil which screens the prophet's soul is lifted, to reveal a man in torment and turmoil. Instead of being models of 'perfect sureness' these passages show us a man wrestling with terrifying uncertainties, locked in conflict with other people, with himself, and, above all, with God. Here is the fruit of a bitter loneliness, of persecution, of a deadening sense of the failure of a life's work. Here is a man wrestling with black moods of personal depression, thrown into a despair which made him doubt whether life had any point. Wouldn't it have been better never to have been born?

> Why was I born?
>> Was it only to have trouble and sorrow.
>>> to end my life in disgrace? (20:18)

a man who often had the word 'why' on his lips; a man who wondered whether, when the chips were down, God could really be trusted; a man who begins a prayer with the startling words

> LORD, you have deceived me,
>> and I was deceived
> You are stronger than I am,
>> and you have overpowered me. (20:7)

a man who could be consumed by the most terrifying spirit of vindictiveness, and go around screaming down curses upon his enemies. There is much that could be said about these 'Confessions'. Let me confine myself to this general comment which is relevant to our theme. Whatever else we may wish to say about Jeremiah, this was a man for whom faith was never an easy option. At times he found that all he had to offer God was hatred, puzzled bewilderment, questions he could not answer and doubts he could not stifle; yet in the midst of his hatreds, unanswered questions and doubts he went on serving God. Life for him was not the choice of heaven or hell, belief or doubt, but something much more complex, more painful in between. Many of us, not least young people, are somewhere in that 'in between'.

3. Let us now turn to that compelling and elusive book, the book of Job. No summary, indeed no commentary, can do justice to it. Let me direct your attention, however inadequately, to certain aspects of it. It is a book of strange, thought-provoking contrasts. There is the Job of the first two chapters meekly submissive, as the hammer blows fall upon his property, his family and himself:

I was born with nothing, and I will die with nothing. The LORD gave, and now he has taken away. May his name be praised. (1:21)

And there is the Job of the chapters which follow, in argument with his friends and with God; refusing to be meekly submissive, demanding answers, accusing God of callous indifference, protesting against a God who

. . . batters me from every side,
uproots my hope and leaves me to wither and die (19:10)

There are Job's friends — and they were his friends; they came to share his grief — so confident and sure in the faith in which they had been brought up. They believed in the justice of God; and in the end they were prepared to rewrite Job's life to make it fit what they believed. If facts didn't fit what they believed, so much the worse for the facts. And there is Job, protesting that what his friends believe does not make sense of his experience. If the facts don't fit what you believe, he claims, so much the worse for what you believe. Caught in the midst of this debate is not merely the question of how to explain unmerited suffering, but a doctrine of God. What kind of God dare we believe in, in this world which so often seems riddled with injustice and bounded with unanswerable questions, the world of the holocaust and nuclear bomb? Your faith won't do, says Job, it's not realistic. After the dust has settled and Job's protests die in face of a new experience of the mystery and wonder of God, there comes one of the hardest

58

and, to me, one of the most biting comments in the Bible, when God confronts Eliphaz and says 'I am angry with you and your two friends, because you did not speak the truth about me, as my servant Job did' (42:7). Can you imagine what Eliphaz's reply might have been. 'But, LORD, there must be some mistake: we are on your side. You are just, aren't you? You are righteous; you do answer prayer, don't you? We have been defending you, defending the faith of our fathers against an arrogant agnostic. We have spoken the truth about you as we received it from Moses and the prophets.' And Eliphaz would have been right. But Job is reminding us that there may be a deeper faith at work in a questioning, rebellious scepticism than in a shallow acceptance of traditional beliefs.

4. For our last example we turn to one of the most fascinating and enigmatic books in the Bible, Ecclesiastes. Apart altogether from the question as to how much the book may have been touched up by later more orthodox minds, the writer is such a complex character that any attempt to summarise his attitude briefly is bound to be, to some extent, self-defeating. Nevertheless certain things seem clear. The writer's motto text is 'vanity of vanities', which the Good News Bible renders, 'It is useless, useless . . . Life is useless, all useless' (1:2). I suspect that for most of us 'useless' will be a misleading translation. This man is not saying that life is not worth living; he is not saying that it cannot be enjoyable and enjoyed. As he well knows, it has lots of kicks to offer, especially if you are reasonably well-off. What he is saying — and saying on the basis of considered reflection — is that if you take a long cool look at life it just does not add up; it does not make sense, it has no discoverable purpose or meaning. Does he believe that there is a God? Of course he does, and the Gallup polls, for what they are worth, suggest that most people still do. Does he believe that there is some divine purpose in life? Of course he does, but what that purpose is, quite literally God alone knows. So he settles, and advises others to settle, for a very commonsense, practical attitude to life. Life from birth to death is a patchwork of varied experiences; and there is a time and a place for them all. We must then accept each day as it comes, live it to the full, enjoy

59

it. But we must ask no unnecessary questions about its ultimate meaning or value, because there are no answers; and he is deeply suspicious of those who claim to have such answers.

'Whenever I tried to become wise and learn what goes on in the world, I realised that you could stay awake all night and day and never be able to understand what God is doing. However hard you try, you will never find out. Wise men may claim to know, but they don't' (8:16–17). The one certainty in life is death. As the New English Bible in one of its more inspired moments translates 3:19, '. . . man is a creature of chance and the beasts are creatures of chance, and one mischance awaits them all: death comes . . .' If you ask, 'And after death, what?' Ecclesiastes shrugs his shoulder and says, 'Who knows?'.

How does all this fit in with the main stream of Old Testament tradition, with the positive, purposive God who reveals his intentions to Moses and the prophets? The answer is, it doesn't. Ecclesiastes stands towards the end of a long, religious tradition, a tradition with which he was familiar, and to him that tradition no longer makes sense. Isn't there a curiously modern ring about this? Isn't this where many of our young people are?

We could go on collecting evidence of the same kind from other parts of the Old Testament, but as Ecclesiastes wisely says, 'My son, there is something else to watch out for. There is no end to the writing of books, and too much study will wear you out' (12:12). Perhaps I have done enough, however, to suggest that what I would like to see is the Bible being used in a 'Life — Theme' study, which we could call 'Rebelling and Doubting' in the secondary school. It might surprise some of our theological juvenile delinquents to discover that as they rebel and search they can find a mirror for their identity in the Bible: that if they have unanswered, and seemingly unanswerable questions, they have fellow-travellers in the Bible: that far from doubt being the opposite of faith, it may have an important part to play in the growth of a faith, mature and big enough to cope with the challenges which life brings to it: that a rough and passionate honesty may, in the biblical experience, be more creative than an anaemic acceptance and pious platitudes: that faith, far from leaving you riding calmly at anchor in a haven of security, may send you out into a howling gale.

Basil Mitchell concludes his contribution on 'Indoctrination' in *The Fourth R* with the words: 'The liberal wants to make sure that we produce rebels; the authoritarian that we do not produce rebels. The sensible educator is concerned to produce good rebels.'[4] In the light of what I have been trying to say perhaps one of the aims of sensible religious education is to produce good religious rebels. They will certainly find plenty of like-minded dissidents in the Bible.

You may have noticed that most of the illustrative material I have used has been taken from the Old Testament. This is not, I think, merely professional prejudice; nor, I trust, a sign that I know little or nothing about the New Testament. It is a pointer to something which speaks to our situation. The trouble about the New Testament — if trouble it be — is that it was produced for the most part in a comparatively short time, in the glow of an evangelical revival. It rings with the joy and certainties of such a revival, and I would not wish in any way to minimise the need for such joyful certainty. The Old Testament is different. It is the story of a long march, a long march across a thousand years of a nation's history and experience. Sometimes the skies are clear and the marchers travel easily across smooth terrain. Heads are cool, eyes are bright, and cheerful songs are on lips. At other times the going is rough. Heads are feverish, eyes are glazed with weariness. The marchers grope their way forward, stumbling in the gathering gloom. Since New Testament times the Christian faith has been on a similar long march. When the going is rough — and it is rough at times for us and for those we teach — do not be surprised if you find it easier to identify with parts of the Old Testament than with the New Testament.

1. See, for example Alan T. Dale, *New World* (Oxford University Press 1967), *Winding Quest* (Oxford University Press 1972); Michael Grimmitt, *What Can I Do In Religious Education?* (Mayhew & McCrimmon 1973).
2. Harold Loukes, *New Ground in Religious Education* (S.C.M. Press 1965).
3. *Moral and Religious Education in Scottish Schools* (H.M.S.O. 1972), section 5.55, p. 89.
4. J. W. D. Smith, *Religious Education in a Secular Setting* (S.C.M. 1969), p. 99.
5. Edwin Cox, *Changing Aims in Religious Education* (R.K.P. 1966), *Sixth Form Religion* (S.C.M. 1967).
6. *Scripture Bulletin*, vol. IV, no. 4, winter 73–74, p. 76.
7. *Religious Education in a Pluralistic Society*, ed. H. L. Puxley (Religious Education Association, New York), p. 110.
8. Philip Rice in *Common Ground*, ed. A. R. Rodger (Dundee College of Education 1977), p. 6.
9. Philip Rice, *op. cit.*
10. Ronald J. Goldman, *Readiness for Religion* (R.K.P. 1965), p. 59.
11. Edwin Cox, *Scripture Bulletin*, *op. cit.*, p. 76.
12. Ninian Smart in *New Movements in Religious Education*, ed. N. Smart and D. Horder (Temple Smith 1975), p. 16.
13. *Common Ground*, p. 9.
14. Michael Grimmitt, *op. cit.*, p. 26.
15. *The Fourth R, The Durham Report on Religious Education* (S.P.C.K. 1970), section 217, pp. 103 f. This report is the most comprehensive survey of the religious education scene. Its brief section on Scotland is somewhat quaintly contained in a chapter on 'Religious Education in Other Western Societies'.
16. James Thrower, *Common Ground*, p. 10.
17. David Easton quoted in *Functions of Faith in Academic Life* (Religious Education Association, New York 1974), p. 73.